Clare Smith was diagnosed with autism at 57. Discovering she has Asperger's led her to re-examine her life through the lens of this most complex of disabilities.

She grew up in Northern Ireland during The Troubles and went on to work for the BBC, where she became an award-winning health correspondent while, with her husband, raising two daughters.

After some twenty-five years there she began lecturing in journalism, but switched to volunteering after her diagnosis.

She and her family moved to rural Norfolk. She lives quietly by the sea with her husband and two cats.

DEDICATION

For Ralph, Jen and Ally, with love.

Clare Smith

OUTSIDE LOOKING IN

AUSTIN MACAULEY PUBLISHERS™

LONDON • CAMBRIDGE • NEW YORK • SHARJAH

A CIP catalogue record for this title is available from the British Library.

ISBN 9781398442290 (Paperback)
ISBN 9781398442313 (ePub e-book)
ISBN 9781398442306 (Audiobook)

www.austinmacauley.com

First Published 2022
Austin Macauley Publishers Ltd
1 Canada Square
Canary Wharf
London
E14 5AA

ACKNOWLEDGEMENTS

To the staff at Austin Macauley who were brave enough to take a chance on me.

And for Thecla Fellas at Asperger East Anglia (a real hands-on, make-a-difference charity) - you never gave up on me.

POEMS

ALIEN

Emotion is

"Emotion is..." he said, "Write about what an emotion is."
But he's taken for granted I can recognise
And I can say what emotion is.
And there's the rub.

The human condition is cradled in emotion,
Is that before there is cognition.
No new-born baby thinks, they just emote
And by their nature show how to be human, to feel.

Well, half the time I can't even recognise
The physical sensations that give the clue
To what emotion is.
In me, instead, they lie.

Oh yes, I have emotions –
Christ! They're the stuff of my undoing –
You'll know them all.
They're the flood that washed me away
This year, this dreadful year.

So fear, and anger, and despair,
And fear and anger,
And fear.
These are, I think, my emotions.

To be human is to feel.
It's not enough, but it is necessary.
And my lot
Don't
Do
Feelings.

Do we?

Untitled 1975

I am unsettled and unheard,
Unyoung, unold – I can't explain.
Chasms of unlight reaching nowhere,
Darkness that trickles allwhere.
Unsound headaches my eyes
Like the unlove round around me.
Chaos.
I can't. Cope.
Choose calm.
Hah!   But that's a lie. I conspire in my own betrayal,
The hiding of my aberration throughout each day.
But unveiled each night to my unbearable self –
Unheeded, unbefriended, my unbearable self.

Plato's Love

I'm too old for romantic love,
Was "unrequited" then, so shove
Your notion, and the reams of words
Written and sung and sighed about birds.
And bees and all that guff that love's a gift
Is kind, is patient – yeah, it needs a swift
Kick up the arse. No, I'm with yer man,
That Plato, who set out his plan,
Three types: romantic,
Friendly – not sycophantic –
And altruistic. But then he ditched
The mystic waffle, and somehow switched
To common sense and, believe me, please!
Decides at last it's a mental disease.

Words from my childhood

Words from my childhood wash up,
Drained of feeling but significant still.
"I am unsettled and unheard" rolls around,
Breaking on the gravel of my thinking
Then, and now.
If forty years – no, forty-one – have not eroded,
If the tides have not, even infinitesimally,
Shifted one grain, one silent cry,
Then let me go. Let the longing
Wash away easy, easy.
Till at last the words
And even the echo of the words
Erase
And leave the shore.

The Meaning

Things.
Things that are said beneath the words,
Heard beyond the sound,
Thoughts not quite caught but still,
Understood:
Being part of a thing,
Unspoken.

Each time I reach for them,
A concrete now,
And I have it, but it falls short,
Pales in being caught.
The awful knowledge weeps in me.
Again, again the true theme:
That needing truth has hurried on,
I missed it.
In searching so urgently, I failed to understand,
Not part of things.

(March 1978)

Don't Sweat It

Panic in the rib-cage, stuttering and sweating,
Heart palpitations - get the adrenaline rush on.
Rudeness kicks in, preparing to fight -
Sarcasm masks it, the Freeze or the Flight.
I'm frightened and lonely, controlled by the feelings
Of anger and failure, despair, paranoia.
And what am I thinking? (If thinking is possible)
I'm thinking how stupid, how useless and ugly.
I'm thinking "oh fuck off!" - I'm thinking I'm vicious.
I'm thinking I don't, I don't want to be this,
To feel this, to do this. I want to be me.
No, that's not the truth. I want to be...
I want to be...
Somebody else.

Perseverance

Per-severance. Per-se-verance
Persevere in adversity. Sever from my sanity.
I am severe. Formidable, they said. Is that good or bad?
Even if it's wrong, it's the right word to explain
What about me mystifies you.
'It's complicated' you said. But how do you even say it?
You produced it – out of a hat, out of the blue - and now
It's out of the box, separate from anything before and it separates
  me,
Marks me out.
It seems perverse, beyond reason,
But in my mind perseverance is not just reasonable –
Yes, it's 'beyond reason' because it's fundamental:
It is what is: I think, therefore I am.
And in the end, it is terrifying in
The finality of the clinical pronouncement.
Condemned.

(2013)

Question

So what am I? This 'I'?

I've got a brain that's been trained to think,
And that's it.
No more that counts.

I've got a body but what use is a body
That can't reach out and touch?
And that's it.
No use that counts.

I've got a soul.
No – I am soul. But what use is a soul
That's blind, deaf, limbless, void?
And
How do I know it exists?

(27ᵗʰ *May* 1980)

The girl who never was

I have Asperger's. And it doesn't scan.
Is there an 'I' that has it,
Or does it have me? From when I began
Did it eat me all up, until when it quit
It can only be said from the process there sprang
Just 'an Aspie': no 'I' in the fit.

Is there even a chance I exist?
Is there some sovereign 'me' in The Syndrome?
This 'me' seems to think, to write down the gist
Of her life, but prescribed by the chromosome
Changes, so the world she first kissed -
For others prismatic - locked her in to a beat of a metronome.

Girl on a Wire

By six she understood, had seen
The blueprint for life, and in a child's way
Had pictured it a wire stretched between
Invisible points, slicing black through grey.
Each step a choice set down just so
In terror. For a misstep would lose her
Into the blind chasm, unheard, and know
That she would fall, perhaps, for ever more
And certainly unmourned.

So she was bound by wrongs and rights:
'Do this and this will follow.'
But such a fear-filled thinking blights
Each step. Each footfall rings out hollow,
And tendons locked for the exact need tire,
Could spasm at any time
And do not flex with the wire.
So it pitches at her touch, as she climbs
To her daily cliff-edge choice –

Her fault. Her pyre.

DISCONNECTION

US Shift

"U.S. shift towards European army…"
Academic essay, complex, quiet,
Inward, under, print and book.
Notes and unheard senses thought subordinate.
"Oh, but love grows where my Rosemary goes…"
Rhythm, music filters through and
U.S. shifts, draining, it fades away.
Music wakes memories unasked,
This sudden push to younger days –
Schoolgirls in tee-shirts and short skirts,
Green and white, outdoor netball court,
Warming up or playing to the netball post.
Someone singing "Rosemary" –
Me? Remembering.
I don't really want to, it's okay
But can't ever be alive again.
It's pointless, remembering, gets you nowhere.
Least of all to understanding why
The U.S. shift towards European army.

(Spring 1978)

Convention

Like nails on a blackboard starting shivers down my body,
Crawling down my back and to my groin,
Her voice grates, unnervingly.
The clichés suit – the things described repeat,
Are dulled by re-percussion.
So, unnervingly,
Unbelievably she says the
Appropriate words.
The effective, malevolent, appropriate words.

Slow-motioned   I sit   quite   still
Appear calm - if somewhat distant.   ~
But oh! The bones and scraggy neck,
The hair preposterously clean,
The mannered pseudo-care disguising her knowledge
She is sure of humiliating me.
Does it all with confidence,
Protected by the lie of propriety.
And I am appropriated.

(1980)

A Life

When Alzheimer's began to bite, he wrote his Life:
A halcyon childhood, a brilliant career,
An honest, brave and caring man, all strife
Dismissed. But among the memories so clear -
And more, in what he did not say -
Lie hints, a different man betrayed.

Raised two of three, he reveals another who died before him,
Who should have been the second, who 'died at birth',
So, not stillborn, not quite. Did they mourn him?
Did he fear he could not fill those shoes that never touched the
   earth?
He said no more, nor of the long shadow thrown
By this most brief of lives over his childhood home.

He sketched his father, says nothing untoward.
You'd take it at face value except that Kit,
Who knew the man, had told me he ignored
His children, requiring only they submit
Entire. 'A martinet' she said, who looked for
Obedience, and nothing more.

Is that why he recounts a picture-postcard childhood
Climbing fells and tickling trout, and everything that's good?
Is that why he speaks more of his grandfather's deeds –
His father unable to meet those children's needs?

He says he turned a peerage down because his Quakerism
   forbade it.
But why then tell at all?
I think he needed us to know that he had made it.
He mentions public figures, a trawl
Of royals, famous leaders, big names like some Bethlehem
Providing safety – he wanted to be One of Them.
And finally, he portrays his love of poetry,
Of Wordsworth, and the line he loved the most –
'The still, sad music of humanity'.

Why did these words speak to him? They raise a ghost,
The child within the man, hiding
Behind his intellect, his prowess, but guiding
His efforts to make the world his home
And never quite believing he was welcome.

Ship

White ship on blue.
Under white scuffs of cloud
Or blue-on-blue scudding through.
But ship as something else, too proud
For relationships or membership?
Those ships trail connections
So fish up near misses too:
This crock of shit.
To which ship will I nail my colours?

The Myth

The Family Myth holds all in its headlights,
Each person and each bond struck in sharp silhouette,
That could cut, if you tried.
That could cut if you tried to creep secretly away.
The Happy Family a bolster heaped up with words –
"Sleep tight", "bye-bye!", "How was your day?"
"Love you".
Each cliché clattering into the vacuum
Of the Myth's blinding light,
All the words, words, words
Buried in beams of THIS version of the light:
That we are a happy family.
But I am in the cold dead centre of the headlights,
And made to see the dark, hard core.

The Methuselah Tree

Dark here, furrowed in grainy earth,
A cell.
A fall of chance became a thing,
A root hair, a root,
Evolving now a tracery in three,
From outwards growing in,
Directly in, towards itself
And slowly burst abroad the earth,
Astride the power nexus
Became the Methuselah Tree.

Towering over its twisting trunks
It grasps above and reaches out
In three, three hundred
Groping and distended boughs.
From the earth's womb
It seeks the belly of its child;
Impotent, it lives unsuccoured.

(January 1980)

Sly Hand Shuffle

How to be Heard?
How to avoid the slip of their sly hand shuffle?
How to trust when you're told
By people you can't help but like "We're listening"?
But nothing comes back - as if it had not happened.
As if they had closed their ears
Closed their eyes their hands closed their minds their hearts.
No. Not heard. The sea-change sweeps away
Subsides.
And across the gulf
Echoes the cry.
Unheard.

Crying Underwater

Crying underwater, tears well and brim over,
But no tears fall.
Each sob becomes a touch
That grazes quietly by my limbs.

Crying underwater, eyes closed and hearing
Muted in this sympathetic womb,
There's still no mitigation,
No reduction of emotion.

Crying underwater, though tears leave no trace
They mark each wrecking ball that cracks
Against the wall put up to protect
Against the knowledge that this is true:
The balm is superficial, the hurt profound.

Light

A childhood dappled with sunlight most naturally
Grew, in time, into a need to find The One.
Each moonlit romance embraced in rapture
And only faded, in time, when children were born
As life swam safe into the half-light of devotion.

Their leaving was as it should be, though a silhouette lingered
And for a time its dark vigil rendered her blind.
What remains is one peering into the night
Seeking enlightenment, insight for what is to come,
Or perhaps she's simply caught, light as a shadow
In the winds of history, facing the cold light of day.

Letter to my Husband

This is what I'm afraid of, what I'm angry about.
I used to believe I had never felt fear.
The odd notch of adrenalin, a sudden deep breath,
But never the terror or sudden small death
That others describe as they let slide a tear.

I've been sacked, I've been jobless,
Been through childbirth and more –
I've been hit by a car, seen my child have a fit,
But these made me angry. I've not looked in the pit
Of fear, become numb to my core.

But what if the anger expresses my fear?
What if my fears were so deep and so strong
And so many and often I could not survive....
So my will, unconscious, took steps. "Stay alive,"
She murmured, "Till you learn how to thrive." She was wrong.

Fifty years I transmuted my fear into anger;
So angry so often, it rose indistinguishable.
It saved me - Oh yes! Gave me strength and my sanity.
A hostile world I met with hostility,
But it became me. I was extinguishable.

But now I strain to change what I became.
What I am angry about is what I fear.
I am afraid that you don't love me, that you'll send away our child,
That I am unloved and will always be reviled,
That I am different – why not fear a fact so austere?

And if I allow all these fears to emerge,
If I show you this sad, little, stupefied person,
Bereft of her strength and assurance, with schisms
So deep the Old Me's out of reach. You'll see what? You'll see Victim,
A type that you're tired of, and I'll be an orphan.

Unforgiven

I have lost heart.
I've worked so hard to do what's right,
I thought that's what you do for the people you love.
But it doesn't count, nor any effort you make.
And I have lost heart.

I lost my heart to my first love, lost the boy and loved again.
Youthful energy drew me on. I sought my one true love
And found him, my armoured knight.
But my love wasn't enough to lower his guard.

I poured my love into my children.
Such a commonplace thing, but how astonishing.
It took my breath away.
And look how I doubled down to do right by them.
I gave them my life, my heart entire.
It wasn't enough. And I have lost heart.
I have lost so many hearts.

FEAR & ANGER

Burglars

They pissed on the bed, ground fag-ash in the silk rug.
They violated us. They left us standing. Stunned.
We stared at what they'd done. Then,
We did what everyone does.
We called the police, itemised lost objects –
The TV, Hi-fi, earrings. Cleaned up their shit,
Removed all signs they'd been,
Got money for the missing things,
Put everything to rights.

But who makes good the other loss – unboxable loss?
Under this roof, within these walls
The things we hadn't counted, took for granted,
Our home, our private place, our safety?

They returned, again and again, those imagined figures,
Reached into my future. Today,
And last year, that Christmas, that weekend.
They're back, they crumble my confidence, haunt my home.

(1994)

Someone Else

My favourite words:
Pristine. Infinitesimal.
Serendipity. Precise.
Azure and lapis lazuli.
Popacatapetyl (for the sound alone).
The words I fear?
Fake, fraud and –
But I don't fear the words, I fear the speaker.
Their intent. Their ignorance, their selfishness,
Their cruelty. Their snide asides.
Their dismissiveness and their dead-pan.
Dead, to my cry: I am so nearly human!
How do I become a person,
Like you? Like someone else?

(2014)

On balance (August – October 2020)

The balance of her mind. Their judgement.
But her judgement? She examined
The balance of her life.
Born defective, not fully human.
Disconnected. Disturbed.
Can pity balance aversion?

Which is to be preferred –
Despair or fury?
I drink my morning tea, and cry.
Sink in my evening bath, and cry.
Lie through the immoveable hours, and cry.
Or wake, and cry.
Other times the storms take me.
I scream and wreck, all too human.
No wonder they turn away.
Pain and hurt. My weights.
Their burden.

Partnership Board

"A piece of work" he said.
"A piece of piss!" I thought and grimaced silently.
Such clichés to hide it's not working,
All the nothing being done.
The ones who don't matter but really care,
Losing out by working out the details.
The ones who don't care but really matter,
Using power to hide the truth:
A piece of cake!
But, in the long run, from the long grass,
We'll speak truth to power:
We'll show them up and call them out
For what they are;
We'll shake our pointless tiny fists, and cry,
"A piece of shit!"

(24th March 2017)

Plant

They use us as a handy trick in movies.
The best supporting, or even the lead –
Cool, with a glitch. The anti-hero who doesn't add up.
You'd dismiss it as lazy writing except
They mention autism. 'Oh yes," you think, "I get that."

They're a music maestro and a maths prodigy,
They kill without guilt. Incontinent killing.
Cold-blooded, but you root for them –
It doesn't need to make sense.
'Ah, bless!' is enough.

They raid us, take a lie and use it to excuse
A hollow figure, a defective character.
So he's violent? So what! He's autistic.
So she's rude? Big deal! She's autistic.
So they're a polymath? Yeah? They're autistic.
And you believe, you get it, you sympathise.
Yeah, right.

They're a double agent, a plant from your world,
But if the actor wore black face, there'd be riots.
So why is this okay? Why do you gobble down the lie?
Because autism fills in the gaps for all that's wrong in you.

The Dung Beetle

She skittered fatly across the room,
Her cheap shoes laced with a froth of black ribbon,
Her malcontent carapace
Past the bulging calves, graceless
In the straining skirt of her workday suit
Three inches too short,
Her thighs too evident for comfort.

She heaved her tiny ball of dung,
Its shadow dwarfing her, its skin
Waiting to be skewered by her ignorance
So it could spill its acid stink.
She does the bullies' bidding,
Has rutted in their trough so much
She doesn't see they scorn her touch.

And so, for this especial day she set
Her ensemble with another confection:
A hair-piece two shades adrift her own dead grey,
Its artificial splendour snapping at her hair.
And barely clipped to her own thin strands,
It nodded madly with every word she said,
The more askew each time she moved her head.

She announced what was best for us,
Despite what we said. Just like her child
Whose genes she denied: "She's simply bad."
She must have told herself her name was true,
That she was a warrior –
Not just a tunneller or a dweller in dung,
For she was the bullies' champion.

Oct 2019

43

ENDINGS

Obituary

Well, that put me in my place, didn't it? Me and all the others.
Not in the kitchen, of course – that would upset the mothers.
No, just a four-word dismissal in half a page.
The rank he held on the global stage,
This man astride his industry. They praised
His bluntness, even his 'brutality', phased
With his 'fatherly feeling for his staff',
He protected all, even the chaff,
'Especially if they were sent in harm's way'.
This, the writer did not downplay.

Well, I'd turned him down gently to spare his feeling.
My ingenue to his older wolf, but I wasn't kneeling.
Then I was 'let go', made no connection.
But now, forty years on and from affection,
My husband says to my astonishment
That of course there was. It was my punishment.

So this obituary recites his work in terms curled
Round one of their own: a man's man in a man's world.
For form's sake, they mention his wife, his second and third,
But what really happened down the years isn't even blurred.
For all of us, the rest of us, they use the Weinstein knife:
Dismissed in just four words: "A complex private life".

A Cooler Breeze

A cooler breeze from a cloudy sky
Whispers around my face, a face that gazes
Away and alone.
Gusts carry lifeless leaves along
And down to the silent ground.
And down to the stony ground.

The window frames my face,
Marking my cheek where I lean so heavily,
And the wind cuts colder when it finds
The tears that cling and slip and die.
The tears that cling and cry.

The air swirls round and through the trees
That stir and sigh to its calling,
And I in my windowless time here echo
The trees and fade with the lonely wind.
And fade with the lonely wind.

(September 1979)

Outcast

Cast out a mistake, a miscegenation,
Mis-constructed and overlooked.
Misplaced by birth to a miserable tribe
Who misread and misled her
Through an uncivil war. Misidentified,
She misbehaved - dismissed her misgivings.
But all the same, they disliked her and left her,
A misfit.
Did not acquit her. Misbelievers all,
They simply left her.
Stranded.

The Spider

And the spider, the frantic spider
Dealing in distraction, hidden for a second
In the table shadow, powerless.
Hopelessly powerless for itself
In the hand of its God, its nature, its future.
But, laughing at last,
It cunningly lays
The fragile last of its eggs.

(10 October 1977)

What do I do?

What do I do with the memories,
My sisters, my brother – my childhood?
Turned out I was damaged, disabled.
And mental, let's mention that too.
The delighted, the whispered, the elephant.
No room big enough to hide its grey shade.
But the sunshine from years lived together
Remains.

Springmount and Hillsborough and Summertown:
The place-names a catch-all
For wide-eyed conspiracies
And piracies and bare-foot teas,
Dock leaves and sugar sandwiches
Of white Mother's Pride.
There was Robbie and Trigger and Perky – his dog, my cat, our
  piglet.
Holidays in Donegal and once I took you camping,
The New Forest a playground for Little Ones.

I remember it all – and the few photos that drift down the years.
Though without them you'd convince me
It wasn't like that.
"You 'remember'? That's just your opinion.
You're entitled. But It's Not What Happened."

You've shrugged away so much of my life
Persuaded me
While your recollections are real.
So what do I do with my memories,
My sisters, my brother – our childhood?

The Witch

"The witch just spoke to me!"
Dismissed with a twitch, a shrug and a curse
They laughed as they left.
She hid and cried,
Bereft.
Her mother's identity flicked into thin air.
She tried but finally fled.
Knowing it diminished them –
Irrelevant. The deeper knowledge
That these taunts haunt the witch, have haunted her
All her life.

Man, Diminished

A man diminished, reduced from Manhood, autonomy stopped.
His selfhood rubbed out, piece by agonised piece.
Incapable now. Even his emotions – pride and nostalgia,
  amusement and awe,
And shame and envy, even boredom and interest – all gone.
His 'he' rubbed out as his days creep by, day by helpless day.
No memories live within his mind –
No mind remains.
No skills that shape, no knowledge forms his will –
No will remains.
And yet he is here. We see him.
We know what used to move him, what he was.
And so we remember for him:
His fight for peace and for food for all, yes, but more and better –
His roses, his being English, his love for his wife.

(For my Father 2018)

Unwary

Do not let grief be the only guide you carry. It is needed,
  sometimes,
For a time, but its eye is poor. It is unable to parry
The body blow that laid you low. It is a sorry ship to hide in,
Dragging through the heaving ocean to some new land.
This will be only an island, not your true quarry,
And you will need, after a time, to let go again.
If you tarry in that empty sand, you may go under.
Instead, try again to compass your way ahead
With a different map, one that chides and harries you,
An adversary until you agree to try again.
And by and by you may find that you have a new thought,
Perhaps only one, one tiny step
In the endless waves of grief, but a mark set down
As your anchor: you may allow yourself to hope,
Or if not to hope, to set it anyway, to let it be, so that one day
You may, unwary, see that you have made your way home.

Cold

Today slopped from its night-bowl like
Long-stood porridge.
It didn't care if we liked it or not,
We had to have it.
So it kicked its heels in the puddles,
Slapped its damp-rag wind wherever it chose,
And even gnawed through the mouldering compost heap
At its warm, close heart, to chill it open,
Dead.

(24th January 1978)

The Bequest

The father was barely in the ground
When it began. The son took the thing he found
Without permission. For who could give permission?
He was the son, the first-born: his by right.
At the graveside it didn't stop. They didn't fight -
They met etiquette's demands. But with their gestures they
Divorced her, excluded her from their grief.
Then at the wake she spoke to one, who, like a thief
Dashed into the toilets as her glee bubbled over –
"The witch just spoke to me!" The mother,
Who had raised this child with this itch to dehumanise,
Oblivious.

And after the wake, the text: "Shame on you".
So squalid that she should rake
The coals of her misery to try to make
Her sister hurt. And after that, the will – a slower dance.
Each child to choose one thing, a remembrance
Of father and mother, of time now lost.
Two chose the same - who would bear the cost?

Each pain as deep, each need as strong,
But how to put right the wrong
Of one to be favoured, one to go without?
So one chose to give up her mother's pledge,
Gave up the ring. Pulled back from the edge
Of bitter avarice. Chose her mother's teaching instead:
Be kind when you are able – it will spread.
But the sister didn't thank her, did not admit this gift
And by her silence dug deeper yet the rift.

Each child believed they honoured thus their parents.
The four told each other they'd protect in death as in life.
In life, they'd rallied around the one who acted midwife
To their parents, as, dementia-scoured, they came to need
Like infants. She'd keep the parents safe, agreed
To care for them. She cleaned for them, made meals for them,

Provided warmth and spoke for them -
Ah, there's the thing: she spoke for them.
Interpreted their jumbled words
By what she thought was best for them.
And best was what *she* wanted.
She kept them safe, so safe she even took
Their freedom, her mind a closed book.

The sixth child had tried to overcome their fears,
Had pressed the eldest sister's case. She met smears
Or silence. For now it was too late,
No parents living now to mitigate
The worst. Or feel the pain
As the four sought to gain
Their parents' things, their parents' memory
And rescript what they held dear -
To be kind and honest, and no veneer,
To ask forgiveness for not loving enough.

What Remains

So much is lost in the shipwreck.
What remains are fragments.
But if you don't hold onto them
The sea takes them too.
And then, what is left?
Just you, foundering.
Seen from afar, a speck
In an ocean so huge
You will never make landfall.

AWE

The Hallelujah Chorus

Gawky and gangly, clumsy and tubby,
We fidget. Stand raggedly three rows deep
In the grubby wood-built school hut
Down by the playing fields.
Sir hammers out the notes
And we belt out the words.
The music wields jewels, sweeps around us,
Climbs as birds convoluting to the crest,
Crescendos,
And
Crashes through us:
"Hallelujah! Hallelujah!"
Everything vibrates. Our world pulsates
With sound so colossal it manifests
As solid noise engulfing us together.

Dawn

She didn't know she woke,
There was merely a shift into being
As chilly night was sifted to become day
And the drape of curtain softened from shaded dark to cream.

But there was, this morning, another shift.
She paused her breathing, thinking:
Something else had shifted, some small thing...
It was an absence, a sifting out.

She heard the quiet, heard the morning
On the cusp of softening from ordinary
To a gift while she was sleeping.
And now she draws open the curtain on the new day
And sees the soft snow, sifting down,
And shape-shifting the whole world.

Blue Bell

Bluebells flooding through the woodland floor,
Swirled about by ferns in scattered clumps
Splashed with tattered ribbons of green.
And inlaid with garlic, wild with scent
So sharply smelt it catches each breath,
Breaks out the unremembered day.
The scent recalls no vision, no day, not the thing itself
But the
        Absolutely
            Etched
                Moment.

So total, so private each pixel tilts at me, each sound comes clean-
  stamped,
Each clear sweet smell spurts in
To that perfect pitch of being, that childhood day,
When a single incised beat imprinted me.
Catches me now and recalls me.
But even as I see it tumbles away, a wake of churned sensations,
Leaving me lost and littered, dazed among the bluebells.

(1973)

The Path to Newton Ferrers

Deep textured pine trees
Protecting the sea bay,
Slate green, whorls
Picked over by tiny birds.
The moss-dampened salt air
Carries cormorants dark-gnarled as the wood.
The birds fly heavily, skirting the shore.

(November 1981)

Evening

My clock ticks quietly, ignored.
The sun sets, a solid rounded red,
Unreflected in the mild grey sky.
It sits a little above the trees
Which grow grey-green and feathered by the breeze,
Among whose spaces hand the bird-calls.
Clear across the swallows cry,
And fling their smallness
Over the nesty, slated rooftops,
The grey and dewey rooftops.

The sun moves lower, now, half-clouded. The clock
Becomes again and dies with a car,
Fading to the distances.
The sun is almost hidden now,
And to remind me, casts a glow –
A pale and warming lilac,
A wash of light above the grey.
Turner would have loved this evening
With its pale grey, pink grey
Sweep of sky.

Time later, the blue deep night
Colours dark mist among the shadow trees.
This vast expanse, defined by the band
Of quiet sweeping light –
Blue, pale blue, pale, touched with pink,
Disappearing into grey, grey-blue
And silhouettes.

Like a star, the street light draws my eye
And darkens the street.
The root-tops now all indistinct,
All blurred and dimmed,
Are merging silently with the curve of trees.
The sky sinks lower, cooler, darker,
Held above me by a spire,
A thin, clear spire beyond the trees.

(23rd May 1977)

Leaf

Spring leaf
Sun lifted
Falls with the wind.

(May 1980)

Summer's Swifts

Screaming swifts swoop by,
A rush of wings whirl winding wind.
Echoing silence streams after cries,
They disappear into dots
In the cool blue sky and then
A lone one swinging back loops down, around,
Gulps air and insects, shrills
Away on a curve of feather,
Slips through the clear
To join the others, fleeing, flinging,
Rushing breaking, speeding plummeting
Greedy living laughter.

(spring 1977)

Trees at St Hugh's Gates

Light and leafy, washed in green
So freshly grown and dappled
With pale-blue sky, sparkling in between,
Caught gently on tugging winds
That carry scents of mown-grass, new-growth, daisy sunrise –
Drawn by dancing birds,
Their fluttering, half-glimpsed, quickly wings
Touching and resting, quivering one second...
A weighted branch...
That springs and bounces, and comes to rest
And grows quite quiet till the wind
Becomes again and ripples it.

(June 1977)

The Worm

Finger-draped she carried the worms,
The grown-ups recoiled and told her to spurn
The slow-flexed things and muttered 'Germs!'

But she, still young, still unfermented,
Hung on fast to each segmented
Beast, and stayed quite certain, and undented.

She calmly accepted the skin all gritty
Was of its nature. She'd only pity
It was dismissed by others, and by committee.

Tramore Beach

We'd lug so much to go to the seaside
And we were a big family – six kids, each
With buckets and bags and parents to chide
Us the half-hour walk to the beach.
A deck-chair or two, a picnic hamper,
Towels and swimsuits, plastic sandals and rugs
But by the time we got there – damper
From weak Irish sun or wet Irish weather, bugs
Biting already, and we got to the everlasting sand:
We forgot our grousing and threw ourselves down
The very last sand-dune to the two-miles strand,
Out past the hard sand, on to the soft brown
Soft edge of the water where the northern sun
Sometimes warmed us, just enough, to cheat us
Into struggling under tented towels to the home-run,
The final mad dash into the sea so sweet, us
Desperate for the breakers, twelve feet high,
Salt stinging blistered heels, choking when we went under,
Splashing and shouting at the very sky,
Filled to the brim with joy and wonder.
And dad, a non-swimmer, hugging the beach ball
And mum, also not swimming, but hugging the shallow
Puddles with the little ones. Ten minutes, fifteen, and then a squall
And we'd be shivering and sluicing, our callow
Need to get dry and collapse onto scratchy towelling
To wolf down a dried out, sliced white
Bread and hard cheese sandwich, and howling
With protest at the hard-boiled eggs, then off with a kite
Or on to the far end, with shrimp nets and spades,
Bowling before the wind to the rockpools
And treasure, or the dune grass with blades
To cut you, but gathering the jewels,
Our buckets awash with crabs and shrimps and
Unidentifiable things. The parents would beseech
Us to give them a minute's peace, until we'd limp and
Grizzle, and slowly pad back,
Back from boundless Tramore Beach.

CONNECTION

Estuary

January February estuary walk,
Marching through the bitter months,
The cautionary outings through October, balk at November,
Till no sanctuary lies along the tributary
At Wells-next-the-sea. The extraordinary beauty
Of snipe and lapwing, their plumage December-gaunt
As they, like us, fight their adversary,
The mortuary winter weather.
But come the spring, which may bring April sun in fits
As goldfinch flit among fragmentary heather,
Revolutionary red and luminary yellow,
Their customary flock out-living the obituary of the sea's savagery -
Come the spring, the emissary days of ordinary walks
Along the estuary, June and July almost in reach,
Then, as some august visionary, we can believe in summer
As some legendary truth, a necessary gift
From this estuary, and forgive our momentary
Drift so that we too could decide to remember
And in our solitary path, walk until September.

The Space

Across a pale sky layered in thin, flat grey,
A thread of birds pull themselves
Free, chasing some distant intent.
They snagged my attention,
Unravelled my thinking for a moment.
But I looked away -
The road, the car, the people to meet.
I lost, then, the pull of the line.
Now, three hours spent, voices slur as I drift
And weave my way back to the thread,
The clear, high note.

Remembering

I remember.
Making love by the fire on my birthday.
Teenagers again, sweetly silly and giggling,
On my sixtieth birthday.

I remember.
Our first kiss, in your car in Leeds.
Your lips so soft, I was astonished.
That touch, the feelings, remain.

I remember
Standing, shocked. But you still walked away
With studied nonchalance.
Each step a knife in my throat.

And I remember
The midwife said "Hold her!" Stunned,
You did, as they tended to me.
And you fell in love. But not with me.

I remember.
You promised to stay, to make your life with us.
And you did. We lived and grew, together.
We changed, estranged or befriended
Down the years. You cared for me.

And I remember making love in the firelight.
You've taken care of me all these years:
Is this enough? You stayed. You've shown me kindness
And compassion, you've cherished me
And loved my daughters.

It is what it is.

Now You Love Me

Eyes closed, relaxing to heaviness and breathing
Gentle, easing wakeful tensions,
You sleep in a depth of physical exhaustion.
Supported in our solid bed, your mind
Disassociates from your body
And leaves now.
Unwary, you are fast, fast asleep...

But now I know how much you love me
For even in this utter departure
Your body seeks me:
A clumsy arm encircles, you press close –
Legs, hips, shoulder, chest and head
Fit secure, and now
Your brow clears and you breath deeper,
Sleep comes acceptable.

(October 1977)

75

Mother Daughter

The love/hate relationship they tell about
Is a cliché and we laugh.
But a cliché because it is so true.

They keep pulling at me, sucking me in,
Batter my emotions with a force I hardly resist.
I have to deceive instead, defy silently,
But I'm undermined, unnoticed.

Then she told how the car knocked her off her bike.
How she crashed into the kerbstone, chest flung on concrete –
And now it hit me -
That sickening lurch, too vivid image,
That cord I cannot deny,
Still tangled in my guts,
Till love beats down my identity,
And I flutter weakly in the aftermath
Of emotions recoiling in confusion.

(January 1978)

Our Time

Black. Disorientated, reaching black
Mitigates to grey, dark and grey. His body
Silhouetted, strong and smooth,
Bearing above me time later.
When he enters me there is no hiatus, just
Warmth continuing, moving, deepening,
A pattern extending from my mind.
We flow to each other, rocking, joining
And create, break, die, become –
Become ourselves again.
Creamy bodies in a soft, grey, dove grey room.

The Stranger

What do you want from me,
You with the stumbling eyes
That light with a quickened touch?
Do you feel what your body says?
Does your tongue mean what it does to me?
Or am I just a lay, uncounted?
I'll reach to touch you any way I can,
For ease, to connect,
For my body to know that you are,
And to find what you want with me.

(Halloween 1980)

A Different Air

Fled the house, needing different air,
Walked the sea-front, ignoring the stare
As I stumbled, weighed with so much thinking
That I am bad, frayed with cruelty, sinking
Under the truth I gave him – and meant every word –
For me. Him cruel? Truth is, it is me who had not heard,
Me - who jabs and twists the knife
And vicious, turned away, too rife
With incandescent truth to hear him.

I'd write of the rainbow that emerged,
And faded, became again and surged
On the far reach, an incident
In which others see a promise. But I was spent.
It was just a field event, of no significance,
As I to it bear no relation, an irrelevant dance,
Unconnected. For what do I matter?
Rather – belonging, being part of two, not scatter
My fears as poison darts: to hear him.

Afterimage

I remember the bright side of the street,
The optimism of job-hunting at Uni,
That first set-back, set to the back of my mind,
A work-around found and a job finally mine.

The Plymouth adventure! New everything -
The pasties, the sea-scents, the spring
In my step: me, a cub reporter -
The elation of covering real stories!
Even held captive by Lenkiewicz had a bright side -
A ticket to new territories.

I careered into my stride up North
And it all seemed possible.
I could go forth and make a difference.
And I'd found love. I was so busy, so secure,
I didn't even notice I was on the bright side.
Prospects opened, sure and overlapping,
Climbing onwards and upwards, and mapping
My way, my sights still set on the Bright Side.

But now will-power drove my steps:
Two little ones to care and hope for -
The world at their feet, scope for the best.
So I took my lost sheen, shook off set-backs
And pressed on. I faced misfortune as others do -
Found a new job, a new home, as mothers do,
Set about finding a bright side.

Then the diagnosis. The weight of it made me limp.
But still I slogged on, scrimping and saving.
I gave up the fight to work - it meant more energy
More time to be with my family.

And then, pandemic. No - none of us got Covid: that's good.
But the road I took is set about with walls
Where nothing shines, no sunlight falls.

So on this my last path, what bright side can I see?
What optimism waits? Not changing the world, not health,
Not work, not wealth - so many nots.
So un-entangle-able.

But I remember the bright side of the road,
So I can imagine, just, a future child
With hope and expectation in her stride.
I wish her well. May she always walk in sunshine
And find within herself her very own bright side.

Gifted

"I owe everything to you" he said.
But dragged by the fearful undertow,
I thought for an infinite moment he meant
The bad things:
His stroke, the hateful words we threw,
The mutual self-loathing,
Brought low by our lost child, and the side-show
Of damage inflicted by disability.

But no. He meant:

Two cats (three times), two allotments, or – sometimes -
  even three;
Good people who now stand as our kith and kin;
The music of John Martyn and Hugh Laurie,
A house we fixed, two houses, three, wherein
To make a home, now snugly by the sea.

And two bedazzling daughters.

Three people, to bring it all together,
A family who need and love him,
And will weather life's storms to keep him safe.
His twelve, his six, his nine, his three
Who stand, always, with him
Held close under the dome of his love,
And who will always bring him
Home.

20th December 2020

82